I0480057

IMPRESSUM:
GÜRAY DURSUNBEK
IM WIESENTAL 3
57078 Siegen

www.ingramcontent.com/pod-product-compliance
Lightning Source LLC
Chambersburg PA
CBHW030945240526
45463CB00016B/1967